ALLEN PHOTOGRA

ALL ABOUT
BITS AND BRIDLES

CONTENTS

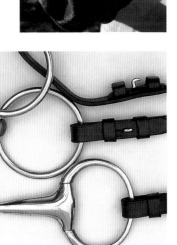

BRIDLING AND BITTING BASICS

COMFORT AND SAFETY

Choosing the right bridle and bit helps to create a good partnership between horse and rider. Whatever type of animal you are riding and whatever job he is doing, he must be comfortable and you must be in control. Some horses may need different tack for different disciplines – the snaffle you use for dressage, for example, may not be ideal for cross-country – but always keep things as simple as possible.

The horse's mouth and teeth must be comfortable and the equipment you use must be in good condition. All horses should be seen by a good vet or equine dentist at least once and preferably twice a year. Discomfort from sharp teeth, wolf teeth, cuts or ulcers will cause resistance.

Bits should be checked for sharp edges, worn joints and symmetry; beware jointed snaffles with one mouthpiece arm much longer than the other. Bridles should be checked for wear, especially stitching and any part where metal rests on leather.

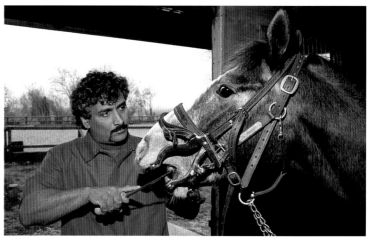

WOLF TEETH

Wolf teeth are small, vestigial premolar teeth with shallow roots which can be moved by and usually interfere with the action of the bit. They are found in both sexes and are easily removed by your vet or dentist when fully erupted.

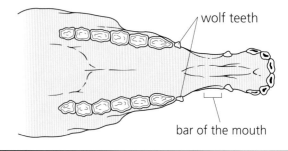

wolf teeth

bar of the mouth

FAMILY MATTERS

Bits can be divided into families. The main ones are the snaffle, the double bridle – which has two bits – and the pelham. Gag snaffles and bitless bridles make up the other groups.

There are a huge number of types of bit within each family, especially snaffles. Some bits, such as double bridles, should only be used by experienced riders who will not confuse or even hurt the horse. But, although some bits are simpler than others and are often referred to as mild, it is the rider's hands which determine whether a bit's action is gentle or strong. A simple snaffle in the wrong hands will cause more damage than a curb in the right ones.

There are a variety of control points on which a bit may act, depending on its design. They are the bars of the mouth, the tongue, the corners of the lips, the curb groove and the poll; bitless bridles may act on the nose, curb groove and poll.

SIZE AND ADJUSTMENT

A bit must be the right size and be correctly adjusted in the horse's mouth. Mouthpieces are measured in centimetres or inches, depending on the manufacturer. Straighten the bit and measure from the inside of one cheekpiece or loose ring to the inside of the other.

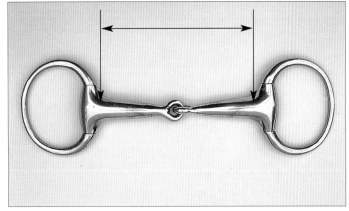

MAKE AND SHAPE

Horses often have preferences for different types of bit, depending on their – and their rider's – sensitivity and the horse's mouth conformation. For instance, animals with short mouths and/or thick tongues may find a very thick mouthpiece too cumbersome. Young horses who are cutting teeth are often uncomfortable and should be treated with consideration.

Too high

To find out whether a bit is the right size, first make sure it is at the right height: it should fit snugly into the corners of the horse's mouth. Gently straighten a jointed mouthpiece: if it is the right size, you will be able to fit your little finger between the cheekpiece or the loose-ring mouthpiece hole and the horse's lips on each side.

If a bit is too small, it will pinch. If it is too large, it will slide from side to side and probably hang too low in the mouth. Bits which hang too low encourage the horse to put his tongue over the bit, which may cause reactions ranging from irritation to panic. This is more likely to happen with a jointed mouthpiece than a straight bar or mullen (slightly curved) one.

The fitting of double bridles and curb chains is explained in the sections covering doubles and pelhams.

Correct

SNAFFLES

Snaffles form the most popular bit family because they are relatively simple to use and fit. Most horses go kindly in a suitable snaffle if it is used and fitted correctly. Certain types of snaffle are the only bits permitted for lower level dressage tests.

MOUTHPIECES

There is a wide range of snaffle mouthpieces and cheekpieces. Mouthpieces can be straight bar or mullen, single-, double- or multi-jointed. They can also have rollers set in or around them. Materials used range from rubber and vulcanised (hardened) rubber (1) through flexible plastic to stainless steel. Sweet iron bits (2) and those containing copper encourage the horse to salivate and relax his jaw.

The action of a bit is affected by its design, the way the horse carries himself and the rider's hands. In broad terms, a mullen or straight bar acts more on the tongue whilst a single-jointed bit works on the bars. A double-jointed French link snaffle has a less direct action on the bars and also less of a squeezing action than a single-jointed one.

KNOW YOUR SNAFFLES

Do not confuse the French link snaffle (top) with the Dr Bristol (centre) which has a flat-sided centre plate and puts pressure on the tongue. The Sprenger KK training bit (bottom) is designed to distribute pressure as smoothly as possible.

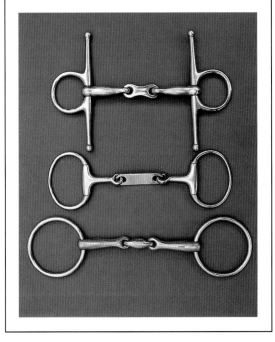

CHEEKPIECES

The design of a cheekpiece also affects a snaffle's action. The commonest are loose ring, eggbutt (1), full cheek and D-ring (2). Loose rings give constant slight movement of the mouthpiece, which makes them ideal for horses who try to set themselves above or against the bit. If there is a risk of the rings pinching, use rubber bit guards.

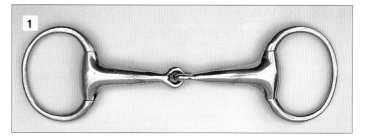

Eggbutts, D-rings and full cheek snaffles are less mobile in the mouth and suit horses reluctant to take a contact. D-rings and full cheeks help with steering a young or ignorant horse by applying pressure on the sides of the face. The Fulmer snaffle (3) has loose rings set outside full cheeks to give a little mobility and help with direction; it should be used with leather keepers over the upper cheekpieces to keep it in place and prevent the horse grabbing the lower cheekpiece.

Hanging cheek snaffles (4) have a small top ring to take the cheekpiece and a larger one below to which the rein is fastened, rather like the top part of a pelham. They take weight off the tongue and apply a little poll pressure and can have single- or double-jointed mouthpieces.

The Fillis snaffle, which allows room for the tongue, has a port (central arch) with joints either side.

BRAKING POWER

The gag snaffle (1) is designed to give extra control over a strong horse and, used correctly, suits some partnerships. There are many combinations of mouthpiece and cheekpiece, but all incorporate special bridle cheekpieces which run through the bit rings and fasten to the reins.

Gag snaffles should always be used with two reins, one direct to the bit ring and the other to the running cheeks. The direct rein can be used as an ordinary snaffle and the gag rein for braking power, which means that the horse does not become deadened to the action and you still have control if a running cheek breaks.

Three-ring snaffles (2 and 3), also known as Continental snaffles and Belgian or Dutch gags, apply poll pressure and leverage. There is a choice of three rein positions: the lower they are fixed, the greater the leverage. American gags work on a similar principle but have sliding cheeks.

LESS IS MORE

Some onward-bound horses are easier to ride in simpler bits, so do not assume that more ironmongery always means more brakes! Roller snaffles are often categorised as 'strong' bits which is unfair as many horses appreciate their mobility and become more responsive. Twisted snaffles are potentially severe and not recommended.

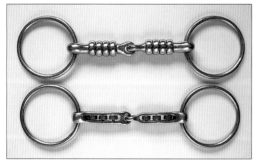

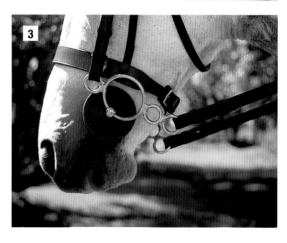

THE DOUBLE BRIDLE

HOW IT WORKS

The double bridle allows an experienced rider greater communication with a schooled horse. It should not be used to force a horse into an out-line or to try to give the impression that a young or unschooled horse is 'on the bit'; a horse must be in balance, be able to work from behind and accept the rider's hand before he is ready to be introduced to a double bridle.

It comprises two bits, a bradoon and curb, sometimes referred to as a 'Weymouth set' after a type of curb. The bradoon is a thin snaffle with small rings and the curb has cheeks which apply a varying amount of leverage, depending on their length. The curb mouthpiece usually has a port (a small arch designed to give room for the tongue, not to press on the roof of the mouth). The double bridle has an extra sliphead, as an ordinary headpiece obviously takes only one bit.

It is often said that the double bridle works on the basis of the bradoon having a raising action and the curb employing a lowering one. This is a simple explanation that is not always true; the late dressage expert Anthony Crossley preferred to say that the bradoon helped with restraint and steering whilst the curb could be used to encourage relaxation of the lower jaw.

THE WESTERN WAY

Curb bits are used on their own by some Western riders and similar schools of riding. However, these riders rely on body weight, balance and neck reining, not on pressure on the reins. There is therefore no risk of the horse's mouth being hurt, as could easily happen if he was ridden English style solely on a curb.

There are many variations in bradoons and curbs which affect their action. Bradoons can have loose ring, eggbutt or hanging cheeks with single- or double-jointed mouthpieces. Curbs can have fixed (above) or sliding cheeks to give more or less play – the Banbury curb allows more play than any other because the mouthpiece can turn.

The longer the curb cheekpiece, the more leverage is available. The Tom Thumb curb, which has shorter than usual cheekpieces, is a good option for horses who are ridden with double reins in the show ring and tend to overbend in standard length curbs.

Double bridles are not allowed in Preliminary and Novice dressage tests. They are optional for Elementary through to Advanced Medium and compulsory for Advanced and above. Doubles or pelhams are used for all but novice show horses.

FITTING THE BRADOON AND CURB

A double bridle should be fitted so that the bradoon is as high in the mouth as the horse finds comfortable, whilst the curb fits into the corners of the mouth without wrinkling it. Adjust the bradoon first, then fit the curb so that it sits directly below it.

The curb chain should be chosen with equal care. The type of curb chain or strap used depends on the horse's temperament and sensitivity, those made from leather or elastic have the softest action and some horses go well in them. Single-link metal chains are not as flexible as the now more common double-link kind. Rubber guards can be used with metal curb chains but are unsightly.

Curb chains have a flylink at their centre, i.e. a single link which drops down, which takes a lipstrap. This thin leather strap is designed to help keep the chain in the right place and lying flat. If used, a lipstrap should be loose enough not to press into the curb groove but not so loose that it flaps around.

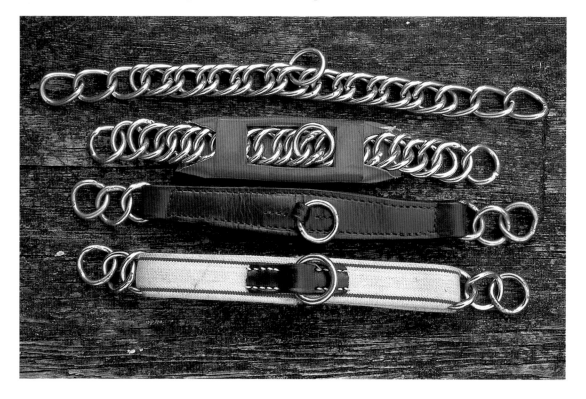

FITTING A CURB CHAIN

Great care must be taken when fitting a curb chain, which is used with a double bridle, kimblewick or, as shown here, a pelham. When using a double bridle, the curb chain goes in front of, not behind, the bradoon rings. In all cases it should lie in the curb groove and should come in contact with the horse's jaw when the curb cheeks are drawn back to an angle of 45 degrees. If it is too tight, it will act too soon; if it is too loose, the bit cheeks will come back too far. In both cases the horse will be uncomfortable.

The curb chain must be fitted so that it cannot twist. Start by attaching an end link to the offside curb hook, then twist the chain in a clockwise direction so that it lies flat and the flylink hangs down (1). Hold it in your right hand, with your thumb outside the last link and your fingers between the chain and the horse's face.

Now hook the last link onto the nearside curb hook, with your hand positioned so that your thumbnail points up (2). If the chain is too loose, find the correct link to take up the slack and hook it on to the nearside hook (3). This time, point your thumbnail down. Positioning your hand this way will keep the curb chain lying flat in the curb grove (4).

PELHAMS AND KIMBLEWICKS

THEORY AND PRACTICE

Pelhams attempt to combine the action of a double bridle in one mouthpiece. What actually happens is that the rein to the top ring gives a small amount of poll pressure whilst the bottom one provides poll pressure and more leverage. The action of the pelham is not as clearcut as that of the double bridle, but many horses go well in pelhams and become lighter in the rider's hand.

Ideally they should be used with two reins, one to each ring. As with the double bridle, the reins should be used independently, not at the same time. In both cases the most usual way of holding the reins is so that the top rein is on the outside and therefore has the dominant action: if the curb rein is on the outside, it will predominate.

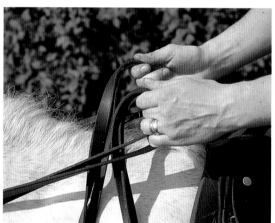

Some people find double reins too much of a handful and prefer pelham roundings (1), couplings which link the top and bottom ring on each side so that a single rein can be used. This gives an imprecise action that may nevertheless be satisfactory for jumping – especially cross-country, when gathering up or slipping two pairs of reins quickly may be difficult. Riding solely on the bottom rein would give a curb action so could not be recommended for English-style riding.

The kimblewick (2) uses one rein and also gives poll pressure. Its curb action is limited by the lack of leverage; the curb action is said to predominate when the hands

are lowered, but a more logical explanation is that more pressure is put on the bars of the mouth. Pelhams are usually more satisfactory.

THE DESIGN FACTOR

Mouthpieces include mullen, jointed, Cambridge (with a small port) and French link. The problem with jointed pelhams and kimblewicks is that the curb chain tends to ride up out of the curb groove, whereas mullen and Cambridge mouth designs are usually satisfactory.

Materials range from stainless steel and copper alloys to vulcanised rubber, flexible

rubber – which, as with snaffles, should have a metal core to prevent it being chewed through – and special plastics. Curb chains should be chosen and fitted following the same guidelines as for double bridles.

Less common but very useful pelhams include the Rugby, Scamperdale, SM and Hanoverian. The Rugby has loose top rings set outside the cheekpiece, giving a little play, whilst the Scamperdale's cheekpieces are held away from the face to avoid rubbing. The SM pelham – named after Sam Marsh, who made it popular – has hinged sides, so the rein action is independent, and the Hanoverian has a ported mouthpiece with rollers.

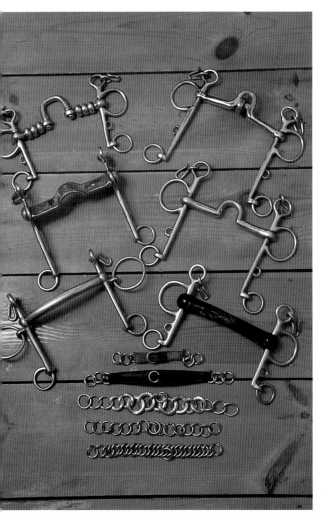

THE COMPLETE PICTURE

Showing enthusiasts often use the Rugby pelham with a separate sliphead attached to the top ring. This gives a more 'finished' look, similar to a double bridle.

BITLESS BRIDLES

Bitless bridles are useful for horses who cannot wear a bit, perhaps because of discomfort or malformation of the mouth or jaw. They are particularly popular with endurance riders anxious to minimise the risk of bruising but cannot be used for dressage or showing. They are permitted for showjumping and cross-country, though are rarely seen on cross-country courses.

Bitless bridles are often referred to as hackamores (though strictly speaking this is a particular design) and all act on the nose and usually the curb groove and poll in varying degrees. The simplest form of bitless bridle is the scawbrig (1), comprising a strap with rings at each end across the nose and a back strap which goes through the rings and connects to the reins. Next step up is the Blair's pattern (2), sometimes called the English hackamore, with a curb strap or chain and metal arms which transfer rein pressure to the nose, curb groove and poll.

The German hackamore, often seen in the showjumping ring, has longer arms and a curb chain and is capable of exerting greater pressure and leverage. All bitless bridles must be fitted so that they do not interfere with the horse's breathing or cause rubs; sheepskin sleeves are often used to provide padding.

BITLESS BASICS

If you have not used a bitless bridle before, start in an enclosed area until you and the horse are on the same wavelength. They are a good way of checking whether a horse is working from behind and whether you have an independent seat – a horse can work 'on the bit' even when he is not wearing one!

BRIDLES

MATERIALS AND PARTS

Bridles are made from leather or synthetic materials. Leather is traditional and most people's first choice, but synthetics can save time and money and are particularly popular in the endurance world. Choose materials which will not rub the horse or stretch.

Bridles are made up of standard parts: the headpiece (1) which incorporates the throatlatch (2) (pronounced throatlash); browband (3); cheekpieces (4); noseband (5) and reins (6). Mass-produced bridles are sold in pony, cob, full and sometimes 'extra full' size, but you may have to mix and match to get a good fit. For instance, a horse with a broad forehead and tapering muzzle may need a full-size headpiece, browband and cheekpieces but a cob-size noseband.

Reins and cheekpieces attach to the bit with billet or buckle fastenings. Hook billets are neater but buckles are safer, as they are less likely to come undone. Stitching can be done by hand or machine; hand stitching should last longer but is more expensive.

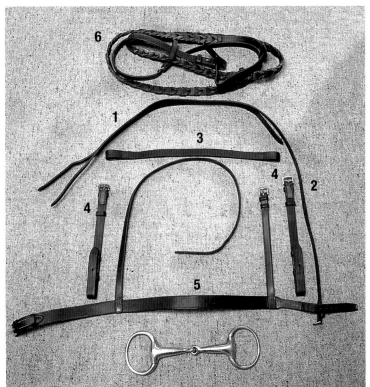

QUALITY CONTROL

Judging a finished product is difficult unless you have specialist knowledge. A poor finish usually signifies poor quality leather, as time means money! Your best protection is to buy from a good retailer or saddler.

NOSEBANDS

There are many types of noseband, most of which are designed to act in conjunction with the bit and give the rider more control. Racehorses are often ridden without nosebands, but riders in other disciplines prefer to use them, both for control and to give a 'finished' look.

The simplest sort of noseband is the cavesson (1) which fastens above the bit. It is the only noseband suitable for use with a double bridle and, traditionally, with any type of curb bit. Some people believe that nosebands with straps which lie in the curb groove may interfere with the action of the curb chain, though many top riders seem to use them successfully with pelhams and kimblewicks.

A broad, flat cavesson that is fastened snugly but not tightly may help to discourage a horse from opening his mouth too wide. A doubleback or cinch cavesson is designed to achieve the same aim and is popular in the show ring (2).

THE SHEEPSKIN SOLUTION

Sheepskin sleeves are sometimes fitted over cavesson nosebands or the cavesson part of Flash nosebands. They are said to encourage a horse to lower his head in order to see over the top.

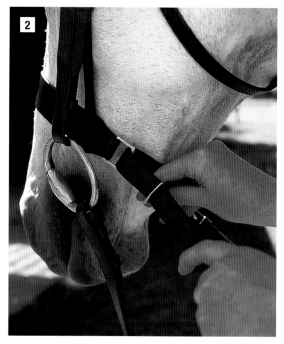

Drop, Flash and Grakle nosebands – the last two named after the horses for whom they were invented – are designed to prevent the horse opening his mouth too wide. They all have different control points and need careful fitting (*see* Adjusting Nosebands).

The drop noseband (1) acts in the curb groove and on the front of the nose. It puts pressure on both points when the horse opens his mouth, which also persuades some horses to lower their heads. Its action is more definite than the Flash (2), which is a cavesson incorporating a strap below the bit. A standing martingale could be attached to the cavesson part of a Flash, but must never be used with a drop because it would restrict the horse's breathing.

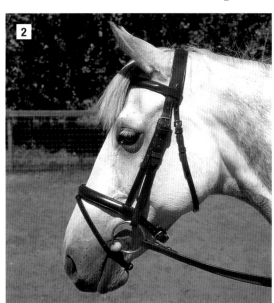

FASHION FAILINGS

Nosebands fall in and out of fashion but should be used for a purpose. Some horses actually resent any form of drop strap and go better in a cavesson: as with bits, using less can sometimes give more results! Flash and Grakle nosebands with elastic inserts are less restrictive and suit some horses.

The Grakle (3) looks like a figure-of-eight, with straps running through a slotted disc at the front of the face. It is popular with event riders and designed to discourage a horse from crossing his jaw.

The Kineton noseband and the Australian cheeker are less commonly seen designs and are both intended to give extra control over strong horses. The Kineton, or Puckle, has metal loops and a front strap going across the nose. The metal loops go round and under the bit rings so that pressure on the reins carries through to the noseband. The noseband does not have a backstrap, so the horse can still open his mouth, but it is effective on some headstrong horses.

The Australian cheeker (1) is made from rubber. It comprises two bitguards running into a central strap which goes up the centre of the face and fastens to the head-piece. Advocates believe that it works because the horse 'backs off' from the sight of the centre strap on his face.

The Worcester noseband (2) is a new design which gives extra control through nose pressure. It has a kind action because the straps which fasten to the bit rings limit the backwards action of the mouthpiece.

REINS

The type of reins you choose depends on the work the horse is doing, the picture you want to create and individual preferences. Fastenings are an important safety factor: buckles are safest but billets look neatest. Buckles are fastened to the outside and billets to the inside. Stitched reins are rarely seen these days, except on some showing bridles, as you cannot change bits from one bridle to another.

Plain leather reins are smart but become slippery when wet, so most people prefer a type which gives better grip. Laced leather looks smart and gives a fair amount of grip, but plaited leather can stretch. Many riders use plaited or laced bradoon/top reins with a double bridle or pelham.

Rubber-covered reins give excellent grip but can be bulky, so choose the width which suits the size of your hands. Half-rubber reins, with a rubber grip on the inside only, look smart and provide security. Continental reins – webbing with leather handgrips – are lightweight but do not always have enough handgrips.

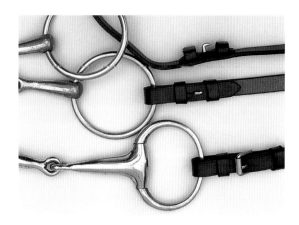

THE RIGHT LENGTHS

Reins are made in lengths for ponies and horses. Too short reins are an inconvenience and too long ones can be dangerous – children using adult-length reins may catch their foot in the loop. Make sure there is enough plain rein near the centre buckle in order to be able to knot the end for cross-country, if necessary.

FIT FOR THE JOB

A badly fitting bridle can cause as many problems as a badly fitting bit. For instance, a too tight browband may make the horse reluctant to have the bridle put on and/or cause him to throw his head up and down when ridden. Nosebands which rub or are fastened too tightly may also make him uncomfortable and resistant.

The browband should be long enough not to pull the headpiece forwards so that it pinches the base of the ears but not be so long that it flops up and down. The throat-latch should be loose enough to allow the horse to flex but not so loose that it flaps around. A good guide is that you should be able to fit the width of your fingers between the throatlatch and the horse's face.

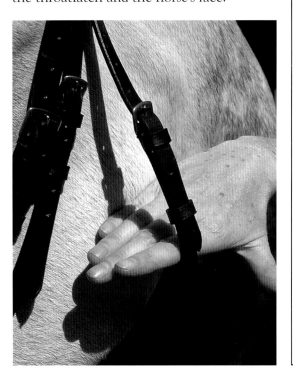

INTRODUCING A BRIDLE

Make sure a young horse is used to having his ears handled and to having a headpiece and browband put on before you expect him to accept a proper bridle. Youngsters are often more wary of browbands than bits. Always handle a horse's ears carefully and be considerate when putting on or taking off a bridle; wait for him to drop the bit so there is no risk of it getting caught on his teeth.

ADJUSTING NOSEBANDS

Cavesson, Flash and Grakle nosebands should be adjusted so that they do not rub the horse's cheekbones. You should be able to fit at least a finger's width between the top of the noseband and the bottom of the facial bones (1).

It is important that they are not too tight: they are designed to prevent a horse from opening his mouth too wide, not strap it shut so that he cannot move his lower jaw! You should be able to fit two fingers between a cavesson or Flash noseband and the horse's face and there should be at least one finger's width between the bottom Flash strap and his nose (2).

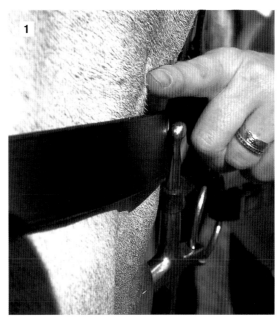

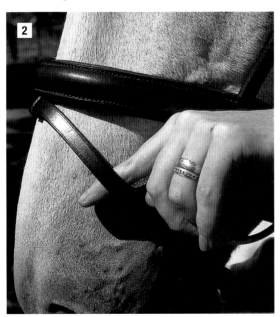

The drop noseband must be high enough not to impair his breathing. This means there must be 3 in (7.5 cms) between the bottom of the noseband and the horse's nostrils and you should be able to slide at least one finger all round. The best designs are adjustable at the front and the back (3) but you may have to get one made to order.

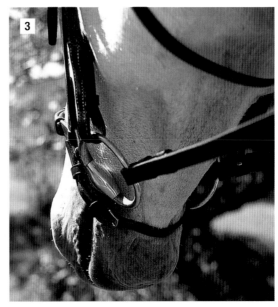

FLASH DRAWBACKS

Some Flash nosebands are too thin and flimsy to stay in place. The cavesson part needs to be broad and substantial if it is not to be dragged down the horse's face. Always fasten the bottom strap so the buckle lies at the back of the jaw, not down the side of the face where it may dig in.

BRIDLE STYLE

The right sort of bridle can complement a horse's appearance. Hunter and cob types (1) look better with broad, flat nosebands and browbands; traditionally, they wear hunterweight bridles with cheekpieces that are three quarters of an inch wide with other parts in proportion. Arabs and fine Thoroughbred types suit lighter-weight leatherwork, but it must still be workman-like enough to be safe.

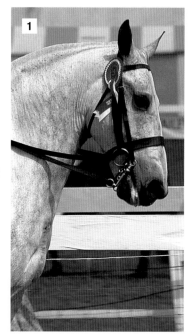

Some people like to use padded nosebands and brow-bands on lightweight horses, particularly show hacks. Coloured browbands or ones with brass overlay are a matter of personal choice; show ring tradition says that show hacks and riding horses may wear brow-bands bound with coloured velvet ribbon (2) but cobs and hunters should never wear them. Brass-overlay browbands are traditionally meant only for driving horses.

If you use a bridle to lead a young, unbroken horse, either in the show ring or to give extra control, fasten the lead rein to a coupling which joins the bit rings (3 and 4). This gives more even pressure: if the lead rein is fastened directly to a single bit ring, pressure is one sided and the horse may become less responsive.

PROBLEM SOLVING

Whilst there is no such thing as a miracle bit or noseband, your choice of tack can help solve schooling problems – provided, of course, that you have ruled out causes such as teeth or mouth problems and incorrect riding.

The horse who sets himself above the bit, or who leans on it, will usually respond better to a loose-ring bit than one which remains still in the mouth, such as an eggbutt. Many horses prefer double-jointed mouthpieces to single-jointed ones.

The horse who comes behind the bit and tries to evade a light contact is often more confident when ridden in a mullen mouth or eggbutt snaffle, whereas a loose-ring style will make him even fussier. Bits with cheek-pieces can help with young or unschooled horses with doubtful steering, whilst animals with dry, insensitive mouths often salivate and respond well to sweet-iron bits or those with a high copper content.

Do not be pressured into think-ing that you have to use a snaffle, unless you are a dressage competi-tor restricted by the rule book. Some horses seem happier with and go much better in pelhams. There are also horses who seem to simply like a change and the best way to keep them happy is to swap between two or three different styles of bit.

ACKNOWLEDGEMENTS

Thanks to E. Jeffries, Walsall, for providing some of the bridles; master saddler Malan Goddard for making the couplings; Face the Music for posing patiently in so many different bridles and Bonita for modelling the Western bridle; Jane Lake and Dave Charnley for the photograph of the Western bridle; Lynn Russell and Kate Moore for advice on showing tack.

British Library Cataloguing-in-Publication Data.
A catalogue record for this book is available from the British Library

ISBN 0.85131.762.6

Published in Great Britain in 2000 by
J. A. Allen an imprint of Robert Hale Ltd.,
Clerkenwell House, 45–47 Clerkenwell Green,
London EC1R 0HT

Design and Typesetting by Paul Saunders
Series editor Jane Lake
Colour processing by Tenon & Polert Colour Processing Ltd., Hong Kong
Printed in Hong Kong by Dah Hua International Printing Press Co. Ltd.